MONODY TO AN UNKNOWN BROTHER

Michael Choniates

Archbishop of Athens

Translated by: D.P. Curtin

Copyright @ 2020 Dalcassian Press

All rights reserved. No part of this publication may be reproduced, distributed, or transmitted in any form or by any means, including photocopying, recording, or other electronic or mechanical methods, without the prior written permission of the publisher, except in the case of brief quotations embodied in critical reviews and certain other non-commercial uses permitted by copyright law. For permission request, write to Dalcassian Press at dalcassianpublishing at gmail.com

ISBN: 979-8-8690-9283-0 (Paperback)

Library of Congress Control Number:
Author: Curtin, D.P. (1985-)

Printed by Ingram Content Group, 1 Ingram Blvd, La Vergne, Tennessee

First printing edition 2020.

MONODY AT THE FUNERAL OF A BROTHER,
IN THE CHAMBER OF THE JUDGES, THE EPHOR AND THE COMMANDER,
PRESIDED OVER BY NICETAS CHONIATES.

Oh calamitous news! Oh adverse and hostile rumor! As soon as it was brought to my ears by the sudden and unexpected conversation of people; they were soon so agitated with such great terror, that to me (as is accustomed to happen to those who are delirious and out of their minds) it seemed to ring and resound, and my chest itself, wasting away with grief, seemed to be pierced and transformed by a sword. From where these tears, I suppose, that are shed by the eyes, have taken on the appearance of those bloody drops, which in tragedies the scenic artist commonly depicts as beautiful: so that it is surprising that I myself have not become one of those astonished and fanatical ones, and being deprived of all senses, have not turned into some column. However, up to this day, I remain among the living, not unaware of the great miseries into which I have fallen, the knowledge and awareness of which elicit these lamenting voices and reciprocal sobs. But indeed it is possible that by this means the avenging Deity may demand punishment from me, lest, being captivated in mind altogether and deprived of senses, I be confined by this ultimate punishment with dry eyes, and without pain, but being endowed with an intact mind, which can perceive pains, I may be more acutely torn apart by being alive and seeing. Whatever is indeed deprived of a sense of sorrow, we say that it is finally devoid of pain. But even if I were to be transformed into a statue, whether that stone, which (as the story goes) sheds silent tears; or that one mentioned in Scripture, commonly known as the statue of salt (certainly sharing the same fate as I, who seem to be nothing more than salt without flavor, therefore thrown out to be trampled by people), still I cannot escape the avenger Nemesis; indeed, I must endure longer punishments, always destined to be the same, exposed to mockery by a hostile deity. Even deeper, the pain pierces my very liver as I contemplate up close, how the wretched end of misfortunes mocks my soul, how the crown of former woes adds to the current sorrows, and finally, how much more destructive and unfortunate circumstances have been added to my affairs: what greater punishment, I ask, can be inflicted upon me now?

Alas, my dearest brother, alas for me! How far removed you are from us! Not just by a day or two, but by a much greater and more distant gap: as far as the realm of the living is separated from the realm of the dead. Alas, how wretched I am that you have been admitted to those far-off places, from which there is no hope of return to us. Therefore, any hope of seeing your children in the future, or being seen by them, is now lost to me. You are so dear to me, my beloved sister, shut out from me. Who will grant me this, that with my death I may redeem life for you, so that, namely, I may offer that very thing which the divine David so eagerly expected, and that too in the son Absalom, who had violently risen up against him, and had plotted against his life? And if he shall not have hesitated to shed his own life, if only he would declare his son, so depraved in character, safe from death, who would not willingly exchange life for death with all his wishes in your name, especially since you are my brother, and indeed the dearest of all brothers, although, if we consider the matter of discipline, you seem to be born from me through the temperament of another's diverse nature?

Indeed, both of us certainly have sprung from the same father's seed, and from the blood of the same mother: and so, being the eldest by birth, I have taken the first step from the threshold of birth, would that I had also taken the first step to the threshold of death, and thus had followed other brothers as one from many!

However, when my father, a lover of books as well as of children, brought me from Asia to Byzantium for the sake of learning, at the time when I was reaching the years of puberty and had been handed over to teachers of the liberal arts, and to those who taught the art of selling (for I had already laid the foundations of grammar and the method of composing verses), he entrusted me to their discipline. Later, when a considerable amount of time had passed while I was there, my father also placed in my hands my brother, who was about nine years old, entreating me to act as a substitute for all the duties of a father, I mean, as a guardian, a mentor, and a teacher in educating his brother. I certainly fulfilled all of their duties, piety, diligence, and while I present myself in their presence, in their appearance, I provide even more than what is usually expected from a brother, finally ascending to the highest level of fraternal duty and piety through their support, and he, in turn, strived with no less zeal to achieve the same excellence of brotherly kindness, and made efforts, besides the fact that he received far more benefits than he conferred, as long as he remained among us to be shaped by our manners and liberal disciplines.

But when Athens first received me and him into the court not among the common people, but among men of primary authority, we immediately ceased to compete in accepting and reciprocating benefits between us. For both I and Athens were aware of many and not insignificant benefits received from him many times, although he received either none at all or very few in return from us.

Indeed, far from being separated by such brotherly love, we were even more closely bound by stronger ties on both sides, and less easily dissolved. If someone had encountered a more dangerous situation that affected both of us (as that natural sympathy tends to cheer people up in happy times and upset them in sad times), one can easily understand how much we were bound by love of country and longing for it, in which we had gained knowledge of various liberal arts through a variety of labors and studies. We had exercised our minds with the subtleties and sharpness of these arts, as I engaged with those who studied the disciplines and mathematics of the ancient peoples, while he, as much as the tender age of a child allowed, was always directed from his very cradle towards pursuing better and more perfect things, gradually training in them, so that he progressed to the point where, like a bird with grown and fused feathers flying through the realm of those disciplines, and especially the subtleties of sophists, lifted by the lightness of its wings, he could now also soar towards those theorems that require a more sublime and noble contemplation.

However, when he had already assumed the manly toga and had reached that age at which one of the many paths of this life was entirely to be chosen, on which he should stand, or enter, at that time, (alas, with dry eyes I will be able to refresh the state of the republic, changed by an unheard-of novelty, and cut with a scar!) at that time, I say, the first occasion of dissension dared to arise, which separated the union of one and the same-minded brothers by different conditions of life. And to me indeed (whom my parents had consecrated from childhood, as the first fruits of their offspring, to the ministry of the sacred altar) private life or especially smiled. Therefore, I asked the Lord for one thing, that I be appointed over his holy temple, and not to apply my mind to such small matters, with which the common people are usually overwhelmed, but rather to spend good hours in literary leisure, and to spend time reading old writings. However, before he had given any certain example of scholastic or of those naked things which are a specimen of knowledge and science. He placed himself entirely in that state and institution of life, which is more inclined to human actions, more studious of the republic, and finally exposed to more cares than is expedient for one who seriously wishes to philosophize. But in order that what he had subjected himself to, and had proposed to his mind, might succeed in better auspices, and more from his own resources, he also exercised caution and diligence. Therefore, he applied as much skill and knowledge of civil law as he could, and the opportunity for speaking, and for acting. By his skill in thinking, as if by a fitting and highly convenient aid and instrument for undertaking the public business, he provided for himself. Indeed, he cultivated and instructed his mind with the guidance of a teacher in political disciplines in the circle of the wisest and most learned men; and not long after, he was exposed to the uncertain and changeable darts of fortune.

This was truly that dire tyranny of Andronicus, which, like a serpent with its many and wandering movements (for thus one may depict the force of tyranny), embraced and suppressed the growing vigor of our empire with its keys, as if with hands, and suffocated it. For as soon as it crept into the sacred halls along with the certain destruction of the state, at which time my brother, who was one of the emperor's secretaries and clerks, then began to breathe a deadly poison and to arouse greater hatred among people than any foul or monstrous beast. And just as a fierce and savage lioness, having recently given birth, is accustomed to gaze at the hunting dogs with fierce eyes, so the tyrant, if he could detect anyone loyal and industrious among the emperor's courtiers and associates, immediately considered him suspicious, and began to strive with all his might and effort to push him away and expel him from afar. He certainly achieved this, and punished as many as he could with one and the same kind of punishment. When he saw that he was hated by the present tyrants, or (to use a more general term) by the enemies of the wicked, he preferred to withdraw from the common flood of humanity ruled by the tyrant, and the immense monster, rather than serve his lust and cruelty; attributing the former to audacity, and the latter to impiety. Therefore, he decided to withdraw far from Jupiter (as they say) and from the thunderbolt.

Then, when the government had turned into tyranny, and he saw that it was no longer open to anyone (who is at least a devotee of true religion, he, with a firm mind, resists it, turning to the study of civil law, deforming the government transformed into tyranny with the muses of the laws, and exchanging it for the shrines of Themis: and what he can extract from the sheets of books through frequent and diligent reading, he transcribes into the notebooks of his heart, and thus finally becomes a living tablet of the laws, and a breathing commentary. Then, with tyranny removed and the revived government, he also returns to the august affairs, as if returning from exile. Truly a work more commendable than so great, that it succeeded the legitimate steps of the republic, the more it seemed to have withdrawn from yesterday's tyranny, or even opposed it diametrically.

Moreover, he was adorned with another magistracy. Although he was not immediately sent to Thrace, to oversee the repair of fortresses, the fortification of cities, and even to have the selection of military orders, he carried out this duty shortly afterwards. However, as soon as he began to discuss with us the plans for setting up a rational life. For the management of household affairs is important, and he who aspires to the control of greater and common matters should first exercise authority in his private abode as in a small commonwealth, he thought first of establishing his own family by marrying a woman of exemplary character, who seemed likely to be a partner in the prudent management of domestic affairs, and especially entrusted herself to the man's care in such a way that the union of flesh and children would be indissoluble through all time, and would provide from such a union that the man would never suffer any inconvenience or harm, as the book of the Wise recommends so beautifully. This practice of his brother being well known to many, how many young men of high standing have tried to bind themselves to us through affinity? Not a few, feasting in a drunken crowd, flocked to Penelope, how many to him acting as matchmakers for marriage; some were planning the marriages of daughters, others of sisters. Some striving to outdo each other in grand and glorious display, and even by a certain boasting of those for whom each one, by the wishes and contests of so many noble suitors, was most eagerly sought after, and to compete most vigorously and to strive with all the strength of their youth and industry, and finally to obtain and become the possessor of them. So some boasting of their lineage, or beauty, or the excellence of both, others, on the contrary, by the weight of their opinions and the seriousness of their words, as if defending themselves in battle array: so that, doubting and hesitating, I felt that a not insignificant burden of duty was placed on me, while entrusting the choice of fathers-in-law to my judgment, and affirming that he would embrace above all whatever pleased me on that matter, if it seemed necessary. The truly brotherly spirit, who entrusted and entrusted me with everything, whose advice would take its own power and effect from me, not otherwise than from some deity! By Hercules, this fact clearly showed how my own, indeed a student of good letters, was inclined to virtue, which he considered nothing more ancient or more worthy of observation than all things in the nature of things: not wealth, not the dignity of form, not the clarity of birth, not the fame of celebrity: although he was of an age that is easily accustomed to such tricks and allurements of fortune, and to grow cold while more diligently and ardently devoting himself to increasing ancestral and national affairs, ennobling the race, and more indulgently caring for and caring for the body than is appropriate and fervently incumbent.

For all suitors, especially those who would speak and promise the highest dowry, not without excellence and superiority of mind, the probity and ingenuity of the illustrious Belisarians, with easy friendship, which had united us under the same roof, under the same masters of the arts as if in a common bond and society, had bound us together in such close intimacy; for my brother, who was very similar to Belissariotis not so much in blood relation or kinship, but in the harmony of character, had married their sister, who had been raised with purity and modesty in the eyes of her parents within the walls of the chamber. And so, like brothers not only in spirit but also in body, they dwelled together in the same house, eating from the same table daily, rejoicing together, being moved by the same things in turn, going to the market, the temple, public assemblies, the palace together; then again, not singly, but in pairs as was the custom, they would return home, each finding the other a wonderful companion, so much so that it was already being said that they were a model pair of kinship, and the happiest example was circulating in everyone's mouth, and so they were hearing the most clear examples of temperance. As long as they lived unmarried, the noble pair of brothers was widely praised among people, but after they were joined in honorable marriage and united in an immaculate bed, then indeed the same person who was my brother became their relative. These others, having been melted together as if in the deepest marrow and innermost parts of each other, began to adhere so closely that anyone would think they had immediately been molded into one mass, which indeed could not be separated or divided by any passage of time, especially because the Belissariotes were considering their city's dignities and the common good of the republic, while my brother not only in the city, but also in the provinces and municipalities, as I have already said, sent by various emperors, presided over the affairs of the state. Indeed, the time was completely open and exposed to change, it took away the empires even while the emperors were still alive, it snatched the scepters from the hands of the Sceptuchians and transferred them to others, and from these to others in quick succession. But to my brother, the honors and magistracies, the continuous succession of emperors, he preserved intact and unbroken, without interruption by any successor, indeed those who followed.

The preceding kindness towards him surpassed, as if competing, they added something more to his former honors, truly men amazed by his virtue, thinking that as much as was taken from his authority, so much was diminished from his honors. And not only common and plebeian men (to whom there is hardly any access to honors, and whose less fortunate and obscure efforts are usually hindered) frequented the palaces. They valued the honor conferred by the emperors at any price, and they sought to add to it with public displays of skill; but these, about whom I am speaking, along with those who love virtue and honesty, compared themselves to him, and spoke well of the emperors.

They were giving many gifts generously and lavishly, and as if some dealers in pearls, unions, emeralds, and precious stones, they were carrying them home at a high price, thinking they would be satisfied if they acquired the prerogatives of dignity at a price, rather than being adorned by them voluntarily. Emperors experienced the exceptional and unique virtue of these individuals, for they certainly preferred to reward Aristides for his contempt of private and personal gain, Hippolytus for his temperance, Bellerophon and Joseph for their sense of justice, and Minos for his observance of the law, rather than the judges who were most concerned with money. They placed them in charge of their affairs at home and abroad, entrusted them with the keys to their rare treasures and chambers, and entrusted their dearest possessions to them as they would to their closest and most trusted friends; finally, they appointed them as great logothetes, ephors, and polyarchs in the open and public administration of the city. By their virtue, as if in a kind of kingdom, they adorned the helm of the cities in such a way that they were rather illuminated by them with the honors, rewards, or splendor of public affairs bestowed by the generosity of the emperors, than the emperors by anyone else. Indeed, to speak the truth, by the emperors in the ornaments of the most illustrious times, and in the helm of the republic to be governed according to the prescription of the laws as if by certain common governors, or masters of morals, were created; such magistrates, once having performed their duties in no small degree of honor, the most ancient Rome knew, who in turn adorned their city, which easily then flourished as the foremost of all. And they extended the boundaries of their empire far and wide, considering the ornaments of their empire as the ornament of the whole world in common, and as contributing to the common benefit of human society. And I will briefly explain the matter; indeed, the bulwarks of human prosperity are safe, however, Pharos and the port, by the support of which they are preserved, have saved us from shipwreck. Yet, how can I so briefly and in so few words run through the virtues of such great men? How can I pass over many things in silence?

Partly indeed confused by the fact that I am moved by a strong and agitated emotion rather than being led and persuaded by those good things, with which they were provided in life and deprived not without great detriment to our age in death: partly, however, looking more cautiously, lest anyone should suggest that this speech, forgetting the purpose of the argument, has made a greater addition than Thylacus, as the saying goes.

Since the new Sion, no less than the old one, abandoned by its own people in such a critical situation, has fallen into the hands of the enemy and has been completely destroyed. Whatever supplement or hiding places or light-armed support there was in it, hostile hands have destroyed, having conquered Nicomedia, the metropolis of Bithynia. And now they are in exile, who yesterday, with the joy of their fellow citizens, were celebrating, today, alas! they mourn with those grieving: those who were once a glory to the city now bring solace to the unfortunate. For they themselves, who used to speak and endure with wisdom and great spirit, brought no small amount of consolation, and with their sharp words they added significant thorns to the courage of those with lazy and dull minds. Therefore, just as

MONODY TO AN UNKNOWN BROTHER

Ezekiel and Daniel exclaimed to those who were losing heart in Babylon, saying: "Our bones are dried up, our hope is lost, we are cut off!" - they refreshed them with conversations, as long as they could enjoy the living, as long as they were allowed to experience both sympathy and consolation, they undoubtedly felt the lighter blows of fortune, and did not consider themselves completely exiled from their homeland, as they still displayed the most beautiful gifts of the city, and even the heads on which the governance of the state rests. For the true form of a city does not depend on hands, no matter how skillfully they may be built by human hands, or on lofty roofs, or porticoes, or adorned forums; but it depends on the honesty, integrity, and religion of the people: whoever possesses these virtues, even if he sleeps under an oak tree, becomes a guest of a better nature, and more worthy than one whom any city, not to mention the whole world, would include in the list of its citizens, completely unworthy of such morals. All of these, as the very foundations of the city, were fulfilled by them at once, as if the minds of those who were the form of a well-constituted state were deeply impressed, as if the laws themselves were animated, and as if they were a kind of bulwark of surviving Constantinople. However, after that pair of brothers, renowned for their holy reputation, was recently called to that heavenly republic, and not long after, my brother, who had joined them as the third of the two, and was performing the same senatorial duties as them, was also included with them.

He was enrolled in the eternal senate; then indeed those Megalopolitans of ours, who had migrated to Nicmam, felt that they had been abducted by them, then with one consent of all, they acknowledged themselves naked, stripped of their former glory: then at last they openly declared themselves nothing but wretched exiles and outcasts, and altogether driven out of the city. Therefore, they also fell into bitter mourning, and if at that very moment that city had collapsed, destroyed by a sudden attack of enemies. Indeed, when it was deprived of all its most valuable possessions, when it saw its very rich treasuries exposed to the plunder of the enemy, how much, alas, Christian republic, the bond was broken!
The unity of the state has collapsed! What a great accumulation of goods has been overturned! What a triple cord of probity and honesty, not even the wise man's pen has broken, nor has it been torn apart by the violence of surrounding events, but only death, dissolving the golden chain of those men, and scattering them individually, has finally

reduced them to nothing: and so that most merciful man, the excellent Michael, the first to succumb to the pyre, only a little remained from that easy and simple soul, as much as the Megalopolitan colony had restored for its own use: the only solace in sorrows, namely that wealthy and highly esteemed John; him, I say, who was said to excel the other citizens in counsel and prudence, and was considered a living example of a well-constituted republic. But after a few days had passed, following this, our colony was also deprived of this brother, and paid its due respects to his funeral, leaving my brother Nicetas behind, whom she praised as if all the virtues of the previous two minds shone through him alone, for whose sake she had also conceived great expectations. And as soon as she lost him in the final shipwreck, today she is worn out by excessive grief, as if crushed by waves, and sunk to the very bottom. On hearing of his death, it cannot be said how great a mourning Asia fell into, and how mournful Europe responded with lamentations, as soon as she was informed of the common loss of all. And if this great calamity has struck both continents as a universal fate (whether each of them had experienced your virtue before, or the fame of your illustrious deeds had reached their ears), how difficultly must they have borne your death, O dearest and most sacred soul to me, whom we, I beg, should we impose a limit on our sighs and lamentations? If we, who are afflicted in countless ways, to whom an infinite number of duties have been added by you, are to be considered in any way of any status or relationship, as I have already said (for the origin of our race is the same), should we, I say, be so greatly distressed?

But the honor of your virtue has not increased, which we do not claim as rightfully ours, when we see ourselves deprived of the splendor of your name, which is spread far and wide throughout all the regions of Asia and Europe, and ennobled by the auspices of your name, we should not be separated at this time, nor should each of us mourn alone at home, but rather gather in one place, surround your tomb, and express our sorrow with the most mournful songs and lamentations, it was not fitting for me, the wretched leader of grief, the mournful precentor, to testify to the sorrow with the saddest harmonies and lamentations by which the army of Joseph, to pay him honorably to Jacob, is said to have been moved. For if we had established our mourning in this way, there would have been nothing at all that anyone could rightly object to us as lacking in this matter. But now that we are separated from each other, indeed, a worthy wife, who is commonly sung about with you, would lead a life of a crow in some corner. And in the midst of children lying on the ground, both those who have reached puberty and those who have not, she, wearing a crown and dressed in mourning clothes, sits and mourns with miserable wailing for her husband and the children deprived of a parent. Meanwhile, the older children, wandering in some unknown places, silently mourn and follow along with a mournful lament. Finally, other relatives and kinsmen, as many as inhabit Asia, have transmitted the acts of this mournful tragedy to those who dwell in Greece. I, the most unhappy and wretched, on a day of great mourning and the third day after, having found ample material for mourning elsewhere, due to my own public and private misfortunes, especially because, entrusted to me, I presided over the very wealthy and famous temple of Athens (that very narrow temple, I say, which is consecrated to the Mother of God and forever needs such a patronage), where I was as attentive as possible in performing sacred duties, I, alas! and with my own eyes watching, saw it plundered and ravaged by impious sacrileges. I, who had been there for almost three decades, as if ingrained in the Lord's court, torn from the altar of the Lord, like a certain lifeless and utterly useless trunk, now, with a stronger blast of storm, am dashed onto various shores by surging waves, or thrown onto some rugged rocks, now, thrust into a sunken valley flooded by the raging sea: truly, an exile in these places, without a clergy, without any celebration of feast days, without a city, ultimately a deserted middleman howls in a manner of a deserted place, mournful, I know not what.

With me, the silent investigator of public and private ruin laments. Now, however, if this kind of mourning about these matters should not be prolonged for me, at least the memory alone will never fade. But indeed, the death of that dearest person, which came like the tenth plague of the Egyptians, the slaughter of the firstborn, drew all mourning to itself, all lamentation, all funeral dirges, all tears finally. For that man who prepares his life for his own wrath seems to have shown me certain obvious exercises of torment, but moreover to have added this struggle, the greatest and highest, not at all free from danger. From which it happens that those former light plagues, resembling pimples licking the surface of the skin, and so easily curable, but let this be inflicted against a certain joy and penetrate the innermost recesses of the soul: indeed, it can happen that the smoke of temptations ascends with indignation against the Will of God, which would herald a future conflagration, and draw tears from the eyes and darkness. after which the fire of afflictions would blaze. However, far hotter and more enduring are those which I now cleanse, as today's day shows, on which indeed the coals have ignited, which seem to me to never be able to be extinguished or restrained from devouring the blood of my heart. From this it follows that my tears have failed me, whether because that water which used to drip from my head has been exhausted by my former woes, or because I am struck by a greater fear, and thus my heart, previously afflicted in a thousand ways, has finally dried up like hay, and neither in the future can such a great stream of tears or a fountain of mournful words spring forth from it, as the magnitude of the disturbance itself requires, in order for me to escape lighter and more expediently once that burden of that pain which I conceived in my mind is finally expelled. Therefore, now with dry eyes and with silent sobs intolerable, this offspring of sorrows must necessarily be endured, and even more wretchedly, after a somewhat shorter span of this life, if anything is considered to remain, I will pass away, and thrown into some part of subterranean abysses, and marine depths, I will lie: and thus to my brother, the elder to the younger, decrepit from the perfect age of manhood to the strength of old age, I will be joined.

O divine providence, which no human effort or conjecture can attain, in what ineffable ways you govern divine and human affairs, which mind, I pray, may dare to believe in and swim in the abyss of your fatal judgments! However devoted to philosophy, can it unravel knots and explain entanglements? I am indeed delayed by the pain that stings me so, that I am compelled to speak such a thing, from which it is dangerous that a mark of rashness be branded on me. How does it happen that I, gray-haired, a useless burden of the earth, who am weighed down by old age.

But why, as they say, should I be nothing but a wound, into which all the destinies of nature have converged, to linger longer as a wretched spectacle in this earthly prison? Surely not fitting for the harmony of the universe, nor should such a fate be exposed to the light of day. He who had not yet crossed the threshold of old age was far more deserving of a longer life, especially by the name of being the savior of his wife and not a few children, having surpassed his ancestors in virtue, and having contributed so much to the common good of the whole world, like a crown of glory and splendor, and who brought something of harmony to my life every day: he, I say, was snatched away by premature death, which almost drove me to madness, not without the common loss of foreign and near kin. For he was not this only, so much good is said of a just man by wise men, but it was also entrusted to us. Where now, I ask, do they live, and those who, relying on the genuine bond of blood relationship, and those who, approaching the same, and under whose auspices they had obtained what they had asked for from the emperors, quickly obtained it for free, finally returned happily to their homes, and expressed much more gratitude for the benefits received than to the givers? Certainly, many or even none of them ever came forward here. Come here, all of you, and with me, lamenting our nation's praises, intermingle my praises, so that we may give tribute to the merits of this just man's praises, and not adorn it with tears alone. For neither mode is alien from honor or decency. Indeed, the death of a just man provokes tears, and makes us labor for his longing: but those who imitate him, seek examples of virtue, cannot fail to cultivate memory with praises.

Where now is that maiden with such a generous countenance, to whom the barbarian enemy, when our Megalopolis was first captured, was already about to commit rape, if this keen lover of honesty and modesty had not seen her, as he pitied her! Without any delay, he rushed upon the enemy, although he could not imitate Phineus in defending her, even though he burned with the same zeal as he once did, our man also burned with the same zeal, at least claiming the girl for himself, declaring her to be his legitimate wife, lamenting being deprived of a faithful spouse, and therefore tormented in the most bitter ways. Therefore, with the gentleness of both hands, he fought with the enemy in a wrestling match, whose mind had been driven mad by love, he drew her to himself, not resting until he had rescued the maiden from the violent hands of the enemy, and restored her to her father. Let her now also be ready to call out for her freedom with lamentations, groans, and feminine wailing, that defender of her freedom, him, I say, by whom she was saved, and not freed from rape, and if he had already been appointed to preserve her modesty and integrity.

What a glorious deed! None can compare with those ancient ones. Hercules is said to have rescued Hesione, when she was exposed to the sea monster; likewise, Perseus Andromeda. But they, armed and equipped with iron, attacked beasts, and finally joined the virgins in marriage. However, he, unarmed, attacked an armed beast, and with so many lies, so many cunning tricks, deceived it, a man otherwise truthful, and not at all deceitful. He eventually restored the untouched maiden to her father. However, Simeon and Levi rescued their sister from the abductors, already violated and defiled, and this struggle hardly, or not even without frequent and intricate circumvention.

With countless murders and the total destruction of the entire city, they accomplished it. Therefore, they should not be compared with our man, who, through his speech alone, without any bloodshed, brought back the girl unharmed and untouched. Indeed, I am certain that my illustrious brother was adopted as a son of Abraham because of his faith. I will not hesitate to boldly and freely say that our ancestors from the line of Abraham were much more excellent than them: for Abraham declared his wife Sarah as his sister first before Pharaoh, and then before Abimelech, not as his wife, just as Isaac did with Rebecca. Those men were indeed afraid to call their wives their own, for fear of perishing because of them. But this man, although the virgin had not yet been given to him in marriage, called her his wife, drew her to himself, claimed her as his own, and was ready to face danger for her, not shunning it at all if the situation required it.

If Daniel defended Susanna from the lustful and unjust judges' fury, and had sat in judgment before them, had separated the judges corrupted by lust, had questioned each one separately, convicted them by their own and his judgment, and had ordered them to be stoned and condemned, thus saving the chaste woman from the unjust sentence. Indeed, he was different from those men, who by nature were so made that no one among us does not desire to resemble him in all respects, not judging like Daniel, but summoning the enemy by the crime of adultery, not pretending a defiled brother like Abraham, not lying about something that could rightly incur rebuke, as Isaac did; but declaring himself as the husband of a virgin who was still unmarried, he deceived and repelled the violent abductor.

From this, it is clear that those things which I am now recounting are far superior to those ancient deeds, for they smell of Christ and are far more excellent in true justice. Just as Christ handed himself over under the name of the Church, even though the Church did not yet exist, let alone be betrothed to Christ (for we were still sinners). When Christ died for us, as the Apostle says; also conscious of the shame he had brought upon himself through his former impiety: "I am black," he says somewhere, "but beautiful, O daughters of Jerusalem"; so also my brother, for the sake of her whom he had not yet taken as his wife, and was not going to marry at all, came very close to sacrificing his life, when he exposed himself to certain dangers, and, though he had pretended to be a man, actually performed the duties of a father, and the natural love of a father towards his children, and his defense of their safety, shone forth much more in him than in one who had begotten a daughter. For the former yielded to the victors, and sought safety in flight; but the latter consecrated building celebrated his annual holy feast, which he saw being honored among all nations, so that from his tent the voice of exultation and salvation, and the Psalter of that just man, could be heard without interruption. Therefore, for these reasons, he arrived at his friends and was brought into the same eternal tents in which they rest, to enjoy eternal bliss with them, and finally now also for us. Boldly and freely with others about the reasons, because he is a loving brother, I am certain that he will intercede, so that he who, just as a bellows does not otherwise than a fire, or a herb or a bath expels filth, we too may be cleansed by the temptations with which we are assailed here, as if by fire and water, and finally lead us to his refreshment, and grant us justification through faith, so that in the same place, as in the place of that wonderful eternal tent, we may dwell together.

The Scriptorium Project is the work of a small group of lay people of various apostolic churches who are interested in the preservation, transmission, and translation of the works of the early and medieval church. Our efforts are to make the works of the church fathers accessible to anyone who might have an interest in Christian antiquities and the theological, philosophical, and moral writings that have become the bedrock of Western Civilization.

To-date, our releases have pulled from the Greek, Syriac, Georgian, Latin, Celtic, Ethiopian, and Coptic traditions of Christianity, and have been pulled from sundry local traditions and languages.

MONODY TO AN UNKNOWN BROTHER

www.ingramcontent.com/pod-product-compliance
Lightning Source LLC
LaVergne TN
LVHW061606070526
838199LV00077B/7191